The Postman

I sent a letter to my love,
And on the way I dropped it.
One of you has picked it up,
And put it in your pocket.

Activity 1

Send a letter to your love

Sing the song.
Play the game with your class.

★ Were you chosen to deliver a letter?
★ Would you like to be a postman?
★ What would you like best about being a postman?
★ What would you like least about being a postman?

Everyone choose a partner and write a letter or make a card to send to your partner.

You will need

card

paper

crayons

scissors

pens

Write your letter or card for a special occasion.

Think of some special occasions.

Make sure you write neatly.

Invent your own postman's sack

Do you think the postman's sack is a good invention?

Can you remember what the sack looks like?
Draw a postman showing his sack.

Afterwards, your teacher can invite a postman to come into the class and you can ask to look at his sack. Remember to explain to the postman that you are a researcher!

Was your drawing of the sack the same, similar or very different?
You could take some photographs or make drawings of the postman's sack.

Find out if the real sack is a good design.
How can you do this?

Activity 3

Designing and making your sack

Work together in teams of two or three like real inventors.
Look at your pictures of the real sack.
Could you improve it?

Think about the good points of the sack.
Think about the bad points.

Look at all the cards and letters which your class has made which the sack has to hold.
Talk over the problem.
Make several drawings of your sack. Choose the best one.

Which materials do you think you would need?

Collect
materials which could be used to make a sack.

Test a few materials. Think about the weight the material will have to carry. Think about the weather the sack will be out in.

Record your results on a chart.
What else do you need to think about?

Make the sack with the best material.

Testing the sack

Get ready to sing the song again.
Who will be the postman?
This time the postman has a sack.

The person chosen to be postman has to deliver all of your letters and cards! Everyone else should sit in a ring.

Think of different ways the postman can deliver his letters as quickly as he can.

Ideas! Ideas! Ideas!

Choose a way and sing the song.

Time how long it takes to deliver all the letters and cards.
Was it a good system?

Did the sack stand up to the force of all the letters and cards?
Look and see.

Do you need to improve the sack?

Activity 5

Can we improve the system?

How long did the postman take to deliver the letters?
Was it a good system?

Discuss with everyone what went right and what went wrong with the system.
Can you improve it?

Try one idea out. Sing the song again and time the new system. Was it better?

Try another way. Time it. Which was best?

Now work in a corner of the classroom in groups of three.

You will need

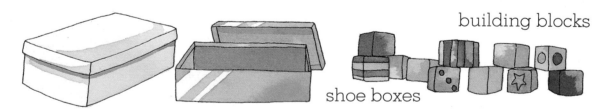

building blocks

shoe boxes

Make pretend houses made out of building blocks or shoe boxes. Place them in a pretend street.

Take the sack of letters.
Can you invent a better system for delivering the letters?

Remember good inventors spend a lot of time thinking.

The postman's route

Look at the numbers on the houses in this street.
Look at the names on these streets.

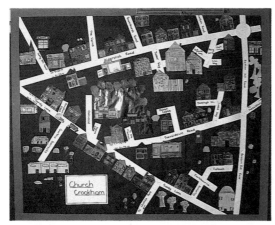

This system of numbers and names was invented to help postmen and other people find their way.
How do they help postmen?

Walk around the streets near to your school.
Find the names of the different roads and streets.

In school, draw a big plan or map of the roads and streets near to your school.

You will need

pens

crayons

paper

★ Where should the postman start his delivery?
★ Where should he finish his delivery?

Plan the quickest route for him.
You could ask the postman which he thinks is best.

Activity 7

Why do we need addresses?

You will need

envelopes

Find out the address of where you live.
Write your address neatly on an envelope.
don't forget the postcode.

★ Do you know what your postcode is?
★ Do you all have the same postcode in your class?
★ Why do we have postcodes? Do you think they are a good system?

Make a wall display of 'Our own addresses'.

Can you find an address of someone from another place?
An aunt or uncle or someone famous?

Pretend that you are sending them a special card and write their addresses on an envelope. You could design a stamp for the envelope.

Make a display of these new letters.
Can you read everybody's envelope?

Sending presents

Problem

Parcel up a small present to send through the post.

The present should be easy to break. You could use a Christmas decoration.

You should make the wrapping look pretty so the person is happy to receive it.
You should make sure the wrapping is strong enough so the present doesn't get broken.

The group or person who invents the strongest and prettiest wrapping will need to test it. Send it by post!

You will need

different materials to be used for wrapping

Think about the different materials.
Test for strength.

Think about the forces the present will have to withstand while going through the post.
What do you think they are?

Which wrappings are best?
Why do you think some wrappings keep the present safe?

Making the parcel

Do you think it makes a difference if a wrapped-up present looks neat and pretty as well as strong?

Collect

boxes   ribbon   wrapping paper
gift tags
cardboard   string   cotton wool

Arrange all the things which you have collected in a display like you see in shop windows.

Decide what materials you want to use to wrap up your present.
Remember to try and not waste materials.

When you have wrapped up your present, think about how to test each present.
Remember to keep all the tests the same.

Choose the best ones to send through the post.

Design and make a special card

Decide on a special occasion.

Design and make a card which later on you could make a number of.

Make sure the card doesn't cost too much to make, or take up too much time.

You will need

coloured A4 paper

decorations

First, ask yourself questions about it.

★ Why is the card needed?
★ What sort of card would the person you're sending it to like?

Have you any more questions?

Plan the type of card you would like to make.

Ideas! Ideas! Ideas!

Choose your best idea and make the card.

Write a message neatly. Tell everyone who your card is for.

Activity 13

The card factory

Problem

Invent a system for making as many cards as you can in 15 minutes.

Choose a card which will be easy to make.
Work with a partner.

Every time you finish a card your teacher will give you

either   1 Smartie for a well made card

or   2 Smarties for a very well made card.

You will need

items on page 13

Discuss in class how you will work with your friend.
Which jobs will each of you do?

Get everything ready.
Set the clock to time yourselves. **Go!**

How many Smarties did each team win? Make a chart.

Let's look at envelopes

Collect

envelopes

Why do we need envelopes?
Do you think envelopes are a good invention?

Make a display of different kinds of envelopes.
Choose an envelope each and say what its purpose is.

★ Is it a good design?
★ Does it meet its purpose?

Try it out.
Can you think of ways of improving it?

Can you sort the envelopes into ones for different purposes?

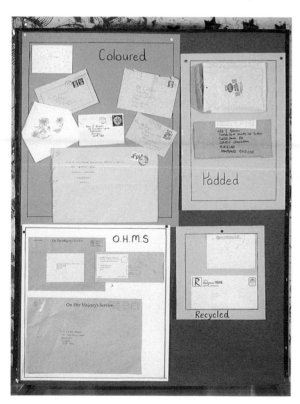

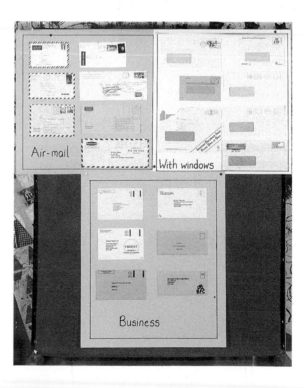

Make an envelope

Unstick an envelope and look at its shape.
Why is it this shape? Are all envelopes the same?

Can you make an envelope?

You will need

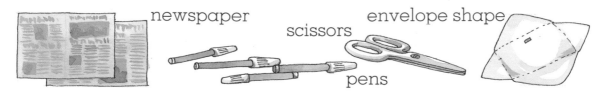

newspaper scissors envelope shape pens

Use newspaper to try out your ideas.
Then make a prototype. A prototype is a model of something which you are inventing.

Problem

Make as many envelopes as you can out of a large sheet of newspaper using your prototype.

You must be careful not to waste much paper when cutting out your shapes.
Why is it important not to waste materials?

You could test your envelopes by putting
your cards inside them.